Peace
and
Joy
Handbook

Indian ancient techniques since 544 B.C

Morality

Author of the Universal Meditation Handbook
Narong Hul
Sina Meas

Preface

Welcome to Peace and Joy Handbook.

Our goals are to help people live in peace and joy by applying morality principles in their practical lives.

Thank you
Narong Hul

Introduction

The moral life is one lived within acceptable behavior guidelines that help people stay mindful while living simple, humble lives. Here, we have created an all-encompassing guide to moral living. Everyone from the layperson to the novice to lifelong monks and nuns benefits from learning and following the rules set herein. These instructions pave the way toward positive Karmic rebirth as well as the path to Enlightenment. More immediately, they help people live honorable and worthwhile lives. When followed properly, these rules keep communities safe, prevent misconduct, maintain the sanctity of life and respect for all, preserve modesty, and promote peace, harmony, humility, and appreciation. A life well-lived is one lived with intention. This book will help you pursue a consciously thoughtful and moral life.

Contents

Rules for the nun

Morality

Five Precepts
Rules for the Civilian

The Five Precepts, otherwise known as the Five Rules of Training, provide a solid framework for living a good and honorable life. When one follows this crucial morality system carefully, constructing his life around this code of ethics, he will earn good Karma and be reborn again as a human in his next life. Committing oneself to follow the guidelines laid out within the Precepts helps one follow a path to Enlightenment. Keeping to these Precepts helps one develop his mind and character, setting him on a path of integrity and honor. They lend themselves to the principle of non-harming in which people think of others like themselves and refrain from causing them harm. The Precepts create a safe community for all and Karmic success for individuals.

The Five Precepts are as follows:

1. I undertake to abstain from killing.

Taking the life of another sentient being is prohibited by this first precept, as it is not our place to choose whether another being's life should end. This includes controversial topics such as capital punishment, suicide, abortion, and euthanasia, as in each case, life is ended. This precept refers not only to the murdering of our fellow human beings but also to refrain from harming other living beings. It promotes a peaceful and loving attitude toward all living things.

2. I undertake to abstain from stealing.

Refraining from taking that which is not ours, or that which is not freely given, can seem simple and straightforward, but this idea is deeper than it might seem. Stealing can happen when someone unjustly takes time, energy, opportunity, or other intangibles from another person, as well as forcibly or sneakily stealing their belongings. Mindful living includes being careful in our dealings with others so that we only take that which is ours to take and is freely given.

3. I undertake to abstain from sexual misconduct.

Sexuality should only be used properly in order to maintain and grow good Karma and nurture wholesome relationships. This includes refraining from adultery, pornography, engaging in sexual activities with those who are unwilling, minors, part of the monastic community, or already in a committed relationship with someone else.

4. I undertake to abstain from false speech.

False speech includes lying, telling tales; this precept covers slander as well as useless speech and any form of communication with negative intentions, which can encompass purposefully omitting the truth or speaking to hurt someone else. Our words are powerful to ourselves and others and should be used carefully. Our interactions with others, our relationships, and the course of our very lives are shaped by the words we use and the heart or deception behind them—both the intent of the sentiments and how they are received matter. Think carefully about the words you use and their effect on others before you utter them. Use the right speech to help and support others and create positive energy in the world and good Karma for yourself.

5. I undertake to abstain from intoxicants.

Substances that artificially alter our mental and emotional state take us out of ourselves dangerously and unpredictably. Instead of focusing on mindfulness, they disrupt our focus, causing heedlessness, which often leads to damage incurred to ourselves and our relationships. Intoxicants cloud our perception and judgment and hinder us from following the other four precepts. Such substances include alcohol and drugs, though this idea also pertains to other addictions that lead to an unwholesome life.

Eight Precepts
Rules for Observance Day

In order to live a more mindful and sacred life, it is important to follow the Eight Precepts on observance days. These observance days can be one day per week, on the new moon and full moon, and the two-quarter moons in between or on special holidays. The list includes the first Five Precepts, which should be followed to live a moral life, and includes three more precepts that provide a stricter code of discipline. This framework is inspired by which nuns and monks follow all the time, but laypeople observe in smaller increments. The Eight Precepts are meant to cleanse the mind, develop meditative concentration, and promote detachment.

The Eight Precepts are as follows:

1. I undertake to abstain from killing.

This rule applies to all living beings, not just humans. All beings have a right to their lives, and that right should be respected.

2. I undertake to abstain from stealing.

This rule goes further than mere stealing. One should avoid taking anything unless one can be sure that it is intended that it is for you.

3. I undertake to abstain from sexual misconduct.

This rule covers any overindulgence in any sensual pleasure such as pornography as well as misconduct of a sexual nature.

4. I undertake to abstain from false speech.

This rule refrains from false speech, lying, and telling tales, also covers slander and useless speech, which is not beneficial to others' welfare.

5. I undertake to abstain from intoxicants.

This rule covers the intoxicants. The Substances that artificially alter our mental and emotional state take us out of ourselves dangerously and unpredictably.

6. I undertake to abstain from eating after midday.

This rule keeps one healthy. Eat two times per day is sufficient for monastic people. It maintains less weight on one's body, which is more comfortable in sitting meditation. Also, one less worry about preparing the meal.

7. I undertake to abstain from listening to music, dancing, attending shows, using cosmetics, and wearing jewelry and fancy clothing.

This rule instructs us to refrain from frivolous activities and ornamentation. Taking days off from vanity and indulging in amusement can lead us down dangerous paths of attachment. Observing this precept aids us in staying humble, mindful, and attuned to what truly matters.

8. I undertake to abstain from sitting or sleeping on a high or luxurious seat or bed.

This rule also helps us ward off attachment and focus mindfully on what is essential in life while remaining humble.

Ten Precepts
Rules for Monastic laypeople

When one commits to the sacred life as Monastic laypeople, they must abide by the Ten Precepts for the entirety of their monastic life. This list includes and expands upon the Eight Precepts. Following them aids in the clarity of the mind and helps pave the way toward detachment and Enlightenment.

1. I undertake to abstain from killing.

This rule applies to all living beings, not just humans. All beings have a right to their lives, and that right should be respected.

2. I undertake to abstain from stealing.

This rule goes further than mere stealing. One should avoid taking anything unless one can be sure that it is intended that it is for you.

3. I undertake to abstain from sexual misconduct.

This rule covers any overindulgence in any sensual pleasure such as pornography as well as misconduct of a sexual nature.

4. I undertake to abstain from false speech.

This rule refrains from false speech, lying, and telling tales, also covers slander and useless speech, which is not beneficial to others' welfare.

5. I undertake to abstain from intoxicants.

This rule covers the intoxicants. The Substances that artificially alter our mental and emotional state take us out of ourselves dangerously and unpredictably.

6. I undertake to abstain from eating after midday.

This rule keeps one healthy. Eating two times per day is sufficient for monastic people. It maintains less weight on one's body, which is more comfortable in sitting meditation. Dinner produces energy that may arouse sexual activity at night. Also, there is one less worry about searching for another meal.

7. I undertake to abstain from sitting or sleeping on a high or luxurious seat or bed.

This rule also helps one ward off attachment and focus mindfully on what is essential in life while remaining humble.

8. **I undertake to abstain from listening to music or dancing.**

This rule instructs one to refrain from frivolous activities that are focused on entertainment. Taking days off from vanity and indulging in amusement can lead us down dangerous paths of attachment. Observing this precept aids us in staying humble, mindful.

9. **I undertake to abstain from using cosmetics and wearing jewelry and fancy clothing.**

This rule instructs one to refrain from ornamentation. Taking days off from vanity and indulging in beauty. Self is an illusion. This self-centeredness can lead one down dangerous paths of attachment to the self. Observing this precept aids us in staying humble, mindful.

10. **I undertake to abstain from buying or selling with currency.**

Those in the monastic community have their basic needs met. Their lives are structured so that instead of earning money to purchase food and other needed items, they pursue the spiritual path. Therefore, they need no money. In fact, the currency would only be a distraction that would detract from their focused lives of mindfulness.

Rules for the Novice
Ten precepts for the novice

The essential precepts that the novice should follow are the Ten Precepts. They guide the monastic community in living a focused and mindful life.

1. I undertake to abstain from killing.

This rule applies to all living beings, not just humans. All beings have a right to their lives, and that right should be respected.

2. I undertake to abstain from stealing.

This rule goes further than mere stealing. One should avoid taking anything unless one can be sure that it is intended that it is for you.

3. I undertake to abstain from sexual misconduct.

This rule covers any overindulgence in any sensual pleasure such as pornography as well as misconduct of a sexual nature.

4. I undertake to abstain from false speech.

This rule refrains from false speech, lying, and telling tales, also covers slander and useless speech, which is not beneficial to others' welfare.

5. I undertake to abstain from intoxicants.

This rule covers the intoxicants. The Substances that artificially alter our mental and emotional state take us out of ourselves dangerously and unpredictably.

6. I undertake to abstain from eating after midday.

This rule keeps one healthy. Eating two times per day is sufficient for monastic people. It maintains less weight on one's body, which is more comfortable in sitting meditation. Dinner produces energy that may arouse sexual activity at night. Also, there is one less worry about searching for another meal.

7. I undertake to abstain from sitting or sleeping on a high or luxurious seat or bed.

This rule also helps one ward off attachment and focus mindfully on what is essential in life while remaining humble.

8. I undertake to abstain from listening to music or dancing.

This rule instructs one to refrain from frivolous activities that are focused on entertainment. Taking days off from vanity and indulging in amusement can lead us down dangerous paths of attachment. Observing this precept aids us in staying humble, mindful.

9. **I undertake to abstain from using cosmetics and wearing jewelry and fancy clothing.**

This rule instructs one to refrain from ornamentation. Taking days off from vanity and indulging in beauty. Self is an illusion. This self-centeredness can lead one down dangerous paths of attachment to the self. Observing this precept aids us in staying calm and mindful.

10. **I undertake to abstain from buying or selling with currency.**

Those in the monastic community have their basic needs met. Their lives are structured so that instead of earning money to purchase food and other needed items, they pursue the spiritual path. Therefore, they need no money. In fact, the currency would only be a distraction that would detract from their focused lives of mindfulness.

Additional rules for the novice

Those in the monastic community follow strict rules to focus fully on the all-encompassing mindfulness and reach Enlightenment tasks. Having them wear their clothes in certain ways and act appropriately in all circumstances creates a sense of uniformity among monks and nuns that ensures modesty, humility, and respectability worthy of their station in life.

Rule#1

I undertake to wear the lower robe properly.
This rule keeps one looking proper and humble.

Rule#2

I undertake to wear the upper robe properly.
This rule keeps one looking proper and humble.

Rule#3

I undertake to close the robe up to the neck and down to the wrist when sitting in public.
This rule keeps one looking proper and humble.

Rule#4

I undertake to close the robe up to the neck and down to the wrist when walking in public.
This rule keeps one looking proper and humble.

Rule#5

I undertake to be well restrained when sitting in public.

This rule helps one maintain his composure with proper behavior.

Rule#6

I undertake to be well restrained when walking in public.

This rule avoids unnecessary movements and maintains a sense of discipline, mindfulness, and focus.

Rule#7

I undertake to keep the eyes low when sitting in public.

This rule helps prevent the eyes from wandering.

Rule#8

I undertake to keep the eyes low when walking in public.

This rule helps prevent the eyes from wandering.

Rule#9

I undertake to abstain from lifting the robe when sitting in public.

This rule preserves modesty.

Rule#10

I undertake to abstain from lifting the robe when walking in public.

This rule preserves modesty.

Rule#11

I undertake to abstain from laughing too loud when sitting in public.

This rule reminds one to remain calm and mindful in public instead of being overexcited.

Rule#12

I undertake to abstain from laughing too loud when walking in public.

This rule reminds one to remain calm and mindful in public instead of being overexcited.

Rule#13

I undertake to abstain from speaking too loudly when sitting in public.

This rule reminds one to remain calm and mindful in public.

Rule#14

I undertake to abstain from speaking too loudly when walking in public.

This rule reminds one to remain calm and mindful in public.

Rule#15

I undertake to abstain from swinging the body when sitting in public.

This rule helps one maintain his composure with proper behavior.

Rule#16

I undertake to abstain from swinging the body when walking in public.

This rule avoids unnecessary movements and maintains a sense of discipline, mindfulness, and focus.

Rule#17

I undertake to abstain from swinging the arm when sitting in public.

This rule helps one maintain his composure with proper behavior.

Rule#18

I undertake to abstain from swinging the arm when walking in public.

This rule avoids unnecessary movements and maintains a sense of discipline, mindfulness, and focus.

Rule#19

I undertake to abstain from shaking the head when sitting in public.

This rule helps one maintain his composure with proper behavior.

Rule#20

I undertake to abstain from shaking the head when walking in public.

This rule avoids unnecessary movements and maintains a sense of discipline, mindfulness, and focus.

Rule#21

I undertake to abstain from placing the hand on the hip when sitting in public.

This rule helps one to avoid an arrogant appearance.

Rule#22

I undertake to abstain from placing the hand on the hip when walking in public.

This rule helps one to avoid an arrogant appearance.

Rule#23

I undertake to abstain from covering the head when sitting in public.

This rule helps one to maintain a proper and honest appearance.

Rule#24

I undertake to abstain from covering the head when walking in public.

This rule helps one to maintain a proper and honest appearance.

Rule#25

I undertake to abstain from standing on tiptoes or the heels in public.

This rule helps one maintain his composure with proper behavior.

Rule#26

I undertake to abstain from sitting with the knees raised and the arms wrapped around the legs when in public.

This rule helps one maintain his composure with proper behavior.

Rule#27

I undertake to be respectful when receiving alms-food.

This rule reminds one to always being mindful of receiving food with appreciation and respect.

Rule#28

I undertake to keep attention on the bowl when receiving alms-food.

This rule reminds one to always being mindful of receiving food with appreciation and respect.

Rule#29

I undertake to receive alms-food in proportion (for example, one part of curry, three rice parts).
This rule reminds one of always receiving food in proportion and being humble.

Rule#30

I undertake to receive alms-food without exceeding the inner trim.
This rule reminds one of always being mindful of receiving food with appreciation and respect instead of greediness.

Rule#31

I undertake to be well restrained when eating.
This rule reminds one to always being mindful of eating food with appreciation and respect.

Rule#32

I undertake to keep attention on the bowl when eating.
This rule reminds one to always being mindful of eating food with appreciation and respect.

Rule#33

I undertake to eat the food in order, not picky.
This rule reminds one to always being mindful of eating food properly.

Rule#34

I undertake to eat food in proportion (for example, one spoon of curry, three rice spoons).
This rule reminds one of always eating in proportion and being humble.

Rule#35

I undertake to abstain from eating from the top of a heap of food. I take food from a site.
This rule reminds one to be well-restrained in eating.

Rule#36

I undertake to abstain from hiding tasty food in order the get more.
This rule reminds one of always being mindful of eating food with appreciation and respect instead of greediness.

Rule#37

I undertake to abstain from asking for food if not sick.
This rule reminds one to abstain from being too lazy to go out for alms-food.

Rule#38

I undertake to abstain from looking at the fellow bowl with jealousy.
This rule reminds one to appreciate the food he has and refrain from falling into the trap of greed and desire.

Rule#39

I undertake to abstain from making a large lump of food.

This rule reminds one to be well-restrained in eating.

Rule#40

I undertake to make a lump of food suitable for a mouthful.

This rule reminds one to be well-restrained in eating.

Rule#41

I undertake to abstain from opening the mouth before the food arrives at the mouth.

This rule reminds one to be well-restrained in eating.

Rule#42

I undertake to abstain from putting the finger into the mouth.

This rule helps one maintain his composure with proper behavior.

Rule#43

I undertake to abstain from speaking while eating food.

This rule promotes respect and self-restraint through proper behavior.

Rule#44

I undertake to abstain from throwing the food into the mouth.

This rule promotes respect and self-restraint through proper behavior.

Rule#45

I undertake to abstain from biting off the food.

This rule promotes respect and self-restraint through proper behavior.

Rule#46

I undertake to abstain from stuffing out the cheeks with food.

This rule promotes respect and self-restraint through proper behavior.

Rule#47

I undertake to abstain from shaking off the food.

This rule promotes respect and self-restraint through proper behavior.

Rule#48

I undertake to abstain from scattering the food.

This rule promotes respect and self-restraint through proper behavior.

Rule#49

I undertake to abstain from letting the tongue out.
This rule promotes respect and self-restraint through proper behavior.

Rule#50

I undertake to abstain from making champing noise when eating.
This rule promotes respect and self-restraint through proper behavior.

Rule#51

I undertake to abstain from making a sucking noise when dinking.
This rule promotes respect and self-restraint through proper behavior.

Rule#52

I undertake to abstain from licking the hand.
This rule promotes respect and self-restraint through proper behavior.

Rule#53

I undertake to abstain from scraping the bowl.
This rule promotes respect and self-restraint through proper behavior.

Rule#54

I undertake to abstain from licking the lips.

This rule promotes respect and self-restraint through proper behavior.

Rule#55

I undertake to abstain from washing hands, which still had the food.

This rule helps one to be well-restrained after eating and to avoid wasting food.

Rule#56

I undertake to abstain from washing the bowl, which still had the food.

This rule helps one to be well-restrained after eating and to avoid wasting food.

Rule#57

I undertake to abstain from teaching the person holding the umbrella.

This rule maintains personal safety from a stranger.

Rule#58

I undertake to abstain from teaching the person holding the walking stick.

This rule maintains personal safety from a stranger.

Rule#59

I undertake to abstain from teaching the person holding the sharp tool.

This rule maintains personal safety from a stranger.

Rule#60

I undertake to abstain from teaching the person holding the weapon.

This rule maintains personal safety from a stranger.

Rule#61

I undertake to abstain from teaching the person wearing shoes.

This rule maintains the value of teaching. The instructor requires attention and respect from the listener.

Rule#62

I undertake to abstain from teaching the person wearing sandals.

This rule maintains the value of teaching. The instructor requires attention and respect from the listener.

Rule#63

I undertake to abstain from teaching the person in the vehicle.

This rule maintains the value of teaching. The instructor requires attention and respect from the listener.

Rule#64

I undertake to abstain from teaching the person who is lying down.

This rule maintains the value of teaching. The instructor requires attention and respect from the listener.

Rule#65

I undertake to abstain from teaching the person sitting with the knees raised and the arms wrapped around the legs.

This rule maintains the value of teaching. The instructor requires attention and respect from the listener.

Rule#66

I undertake to abstain from teaching the person wearing a hat.

This rule maintains the value of teaching. The instructor requires attention and respect from the listener.

Rule#67

I undertake to abstain from teaching the person wearing the scarf to cover the head.

This rule maintains the value of teaching. The instructor requires attention and respect from the listener.

Rule#68

I undertake to abstain from teaching the person sitting on the seat while I'm sitting on the ground.
This rule maintains the value of teaching. The instructor requires attention and respect from the listener.

Rule#69

I undertake to abstain from teaching the person sitting on the high chair while I'm sitting on a lower chair.
This rule maintains the value of teaching. The instructor requires attention and respect from the listener.

Rule#70

I undertake to abstain from teaching the person who is sitting while I'm standing.
This rule maintains the value of teaching. The instructor requires attention and respect from the listener.

Rule#71

I undertake to abstain from teaching the person who is walking ahead.
This rule maintains the value of teaching. The instructor requires attention and respect from the listener.

Rule#72

I undertake to abstain from teaching the person walking on the pathway while I walk on the sideway.
This rule maintains the value of teaching. The instructor requires attention and respect from the listener.

Rule#73

I undertake to abstain from defecating or urinating while standing.
This rule preserves modesty.

Rule#74

I undertake to abstain from defecating or urinating, or spitting on the living plants.
All life is sacred, including plants. They, therefore, deserve to be respected.

Rule#75

I undertake to abstain from defecating or urinating, or spitting into the water.
This rule prevents one from contaminating water fit for drinking or bathing. Not only does it promote good hygiene and healthy living, but it is also a matter of respect.

Rules for the monk
Four precepts for the monk

1. I'm well restrained to the rules of conduct.

Monastic life requires its members to both practices good, helpful acts and avoid bad behavior to live purely and focus on the path to Enlightenment. This involves strictly adhering to a set of rules that promote a life that is humble, proper, respectful, and mindful.

2. I restrain my eyes, ears, nose, mouth, body, and emotion.

From his body to his mind, every part of the monk should maintain focus on his path. This means that no part of himself should create or give into desires or feelings of hatred.

3. I live with the right livelihood.

Monks are expected to live wholesome lives in which they perform only good acts and are respectful at all times of all life, and mindful of the rules set out for them. This includes regarding all life as sacred, harming no being, speaking only the truth, and refraining from misleading or seducing others.

4. **I contemplate the four offerings (food, medicine, robe, and shelter).**

Monks are expected to contemplate the four offerings, which are the necessities required for basic life. In this contemplation, they should refrain from attachment and desire while mindfully respecting and appreciating the offerings that keep them alive and allow them the freedom to follow their path with their basic needs met.

Additional 227 rules for the monk
First-degree misconduct

Rule#1

I undertake to abstain from sexual contact with humans or animals.

Sexuality is a powerful force, one that is easy to get pulled into. Monks need to remain chaste to focus their energy on their path and resist the pull of desire.

Rule#2

I undertake to abstain from stealing.

The mindful and moral life of monks includes being careful in their dealings with others only to take theirs and are freely given.

Rule#3

I undertake to abstain from killing a human.

Human life is sacred. It is no one's place to judge another life or decide who gets to live or die.

Rule#4

I undertake to abstain from the false claim of high attainment achievement.

Words are powerful to ourselves and others, creating the course of our lives and relationships. They should, therefore, be used carefully. Truth is precious and should be adhered to at all times.

Second-degree misconduct

Rule#1

I undertake to abstain from masturbation.
This rule helps monks stay calm and mindful instead of forming attachments to the physical world and getting lost in desire.

Rule#2

I undertake to abstain from physically contacting the woman with lust.
Sexuality is a powerful force, one that is easy to get pulled into. Monks need to remain chaste and virtuous so they can focus their energy on their path and resist the pull of desire. This includes abstaining from any act that leads one to think of or desire to engage in sexual thoughts or acts.

Rule#3

I undertake to abstain from flirting with a woman.
Though flirting might seem like an innocent act, it is the first step that leads to sexual thoughts and activity. This rule helps monks maintain a virtuous mind.

Rule#4

I undertake to abstain from seducing a woman for sex.
This rule helps maintain chastity and avoids any potential for or suspicions of misconduct, beyond a doubt, with those of the opposite sex.

Rule#5

I undertake to abstain from engaging the man with a woman.
This rule helps avoid arranging the marriage.

Rule#6

I undertake to abstain from asking someone to make a shelter larger than (3m x 1.75m) for me without administrator approval.
This rule helps avoid attachment to the materials and exploiting the laypeople.

Rule#7

I undertake to abstain from asking someone to make a building for me without administrator approval.
This rule helps avoid attachment to the materials and exploiting the laypeople.

Rule#8

I undertake to abstain from accusing the fellow of serious misconduct without clear evidence.
This rule helps maintain peace and harmony in the monastery.

Rule#9

I undertake to abstain from accusing the fellow of serious misconduct with exaggerated false claims.
This rule helps maintain peace and harmony in the monastery.

Rule#10

I undertake to abstain from creating a division in the monastery.
This rule helps maintain peace and harmony in the monastery.

Rule#11

I undertake to abstain from participating with others to create a division in the monastery.
This rule helps maintain peace and harmony in the monastery.

Rule#12

I undertake to abstain from defying the judgment of the administrator.
This rule helps maintain a level of respect and order within the monastery.

Rule#13

I undertake to abstain from exploiting the laypeople.
This rule helps gain trust and respect from laypeople.

Third-degree misconduct

Rule#1

I undertake to abstain from being in private with a woman, which creates doubt of sexual contact.
This rule helps maintain chastity and avoids any potential for or suspicions of misconduct, beyond a doubt with those of the opposite sex.

Rule#2

I undertake to abstain from being in private with a woman, which creates doubt of flirting.
Though flirting might seem like an innocent act, it is the first step that leads to sexual thoughts and activity. This rule helps monks maintain a virtuous mind.

Fourth-degree misconduct

Rule#1

I undertake to abstain from keeping the extra robes for more than ten days. (3 robes are permitted)
This rule helps avoid attachment to the materials.

Rule#2

I undertake to abstain from sleeping far from the robes.
This rule helps prevent misplacing one's robes.

Rule#3

I undertake to abstain from keeping cloth to make new robe than one month.
This rule helps avoid attachment to the materials.

Rule#4

I undertake to abstain from asking a non-relative nun to wash or dye the robe.
This rule keeps one from improper contact with the opposite sex.

Rule#5

I undertake to abstain from receiving the robe from the non-relative nun.
This rule keeps one from improper contact with the opposite sex.

Rule#6

I undertake to abstain from asking non-relative lay-people for a robe.

This rule prevents the exploitation of laypeople.

Rule#7

I undertake to abstain from asking for more than one set of the robe in case of losing all the three robes.

This rule prevents the exploitation of laypeople.

Rule#8

I undertake to abstain from asking laypeople for the finest robe.

This rule prevents the exploitation of laypeople.

Rule#9

I undertake to abstain from asking another layperson of an extra finest robe.

This rule prevents the exploitation of laypeople.

Rule#10

I undertake to abstain from asking the assistance (the money keeper) for an essential item more than three times, not stand in front of him more than six times. If I do not get the item, I inform the donor to get their money back from the assistance.

This rule keeps everyone honest and accountable.

Rule#11

I undertake to abstain from accepting the silk carpet.
This rule helps avoid attachment to the materials.

Rule#12

I undertake to abstain from accepting the carpet made of 100percent black sheep wool.
This rule helps avoid attachment to the materials.

Rule#13

I undertake to abstain from accepting the carpet made of black sheep wool and the white sheep wool.
This rule helps avoid attachment to the materials.

Rule#14

I undertake to abstain from accepting the new carpet unless the old one is over six years old.
This rule helps avoid attachment to the materials.

Rule#15

I undertake to abstain from using the new carpet without some part of the old one.
This rule helps avoid attachment to the materials.

Rule#16

I undertake to abstain from carrying the raw wool for more than three walking days (48km).
This rule avoids attachment to the materials.

Rule#17

I undertake to abstain from asking the monk or nun to wash, dye the wool.

This rule prevents the exploitation of the fellow.

Rule#18

I undertake to abstain from accepting the money.

Those in the monastic community have their basic needs met. Therefore, they need no money.

Rule#19

I undertake to abstain from handling the money.

Those in the monastic community have their basic needs met. Therefore, they need no money.

Rule#20

I undertake to abstain from exchange things.

Those in the monastic community have their basic needs met.

Rule#21

I undertake to abstain from keeping an extra bowl (food container) for more than ten days.

This rule helps those in the monastic community avoid attachment to the materials.

Rule#22

I undertake to abstain from asking for a new bowl (food container) unless the old one was broken or unusable.

This rule helps those in the monastic community avoid attachment to the materials.

Rule#23

I undertake to abstain from keeping the food as medicine for more than seven days.

This rule promotes healthy living through proper food usage.

Rule#24

I undertake to abstain from receiving the rain robe long before the rainy retreat season.

This rule promotes humility and prevents attachment to materials.

Rule#25

I undertake to abstain from taking back the robe after giving it away.

This rule keeps everyone honest and accountable.

Rule#26

I undertake to abstain from making the finest robe for myself.

This rule helps those in the monastic community avoid attachment to the materials.

Rule#27

I undertake to abstain from ordering the finest robe.

This rule helps those in the monastic community avoid attachment to the materials.

Rule#28

I undertake to abstain from accepting the extra robe unless authorized.

This rule helps those in the monastic community avoid attachment to the materials.

Rule#29

I undertake to abstain from leaving the robe for more than six nights. (except the rainy retreat season).

This rule prevents one from losing the robe.

Rule#30

I undertake to abstain from diverting the donation to myself if it's intended for all the fellow.

This rule keeps everyone honest and accountable.

Fifth-degree misconduct

Rule#1

I undertake to abstain from lying.
This rule helps monks preserve the sanctity of truth while also keeping them virtuous.

Rule#2

I undertake to abstain from insulting another fellow.
This rule helps maintain peace among fellow and reminds one to treat others with kindness.

Rule#3

I undertake to abstain from arguing with another fellow.
This rule helps maintain peace among fellow and reminds one to treat others with kindness.

Rule#4

I undertake to abstain from reciting the text with the laypeople.
The monkhood is sacred. This rule helps maintain its sanctity.

<h1 style="text-align:center">Rule#5</h1>

I undertake to abstain from sleeping in the same building with laypeople for more than three nights.
This rule prevents laypeople's exploitation and ensures that monks realize that their home is in the monastery instead of out in the world with laypeople.

<h1 style="text-align:center">Rule#6</h1>

I undertake to abstain from lying down in the building where the woman is also there.
This rule ensures no opportunity for sexual or behavioral misconduct with those of the opposite sex and no opportunity to suspect it.

<h1 style="text-align:center">Rule#7</h1>

I undertake to abstain from teaching the woman without the presence of another man.
This rule ensures no opportunity for sexual or behavioral misconduct with those of the opposite sex and no opportunity to suspect it.

<h1 style="text-align:center">Rule#8</h1>

I undertake to abstain from telling the achievement of attainment to laypeople.
This rule helps maintain humility and avoid bragging.

Rule#9

I undertake to abstain from revealing the severe misconduct of the fellow to the laypeople.

This rule protects the fellows and the monastery as a whole from outside suspicion and trouble. People, including monks, will always make mistakes, but they can learn from them and grow not to commit the offense again. There is no need to involved the outside community in the inner affairs of the monastery.

Rule#10

I undertake to abstain from digging the ground or ask someone to do it.

This rule is a reminder that all life is sacred and should be treated as such, including plants and small creatures.

Rule#11

I undertake to abstain from damaging the living plants.

This rule is a reminder that all life is sacred and should be treated as such, including plants.

Rule#12

I undertake to abstain from finding the fault of the administrator.

This rule helps maintain a level of respect and order within the monastery.

Rule#13

I undertake to abstain from criticizing the fellow.
This rule helps maintain peace and harmony in the monastery.

Rule#14

I undertake to abstain from using a chair or bed in public, then leave without returning it to a proper place.
This rule helps keep the public in proper order.

Rule#15

I undertake to abstain from using a chair or bed in the monastery, then leave without returning it to a proper place.
This rule helps keep the monastery in proper order.

Rule#16

I undertake to abstain from intruding the occupied dwelling.
This rule helps maintain peace and harmony in the monastery.

Rule#17

I undertake to abstain from expelling the roommate from the dwelling.
This rule is a reminder for monks to be kind and thoughtful to their fellows.

Rule#18

I undertake to abstain from using the bed or chair, which is not ready for use.

This rule keeps everyone safe from injury.

Rule#19

I undertake to abstain from building a roof with more than three layers.

This rule keeps everyone safe from injury.

Rule#20

I undertake to abstain from pouring the water containing the insect.

All life is sacred and should be treated as such, even the smallest creatures such as insects.

Rule#21

I undertake to abstain from teaching the nun without the approval of the administrator.

This rule ensures no opportunity for sexual or behavioral misconduct with those of the opposite sex and no opportunity to suspect it.

Rule#22

I undertake to abstain from teaching the nun after sunset.
This rule ensures no opportunity for sexual or behavioral misconduct with those of the opposite sex and no opportunity to suspect it.

Rule#23

I undertake to abstain from going to the nun dwelling for teaching.
This rule ensures no opportunity for sexual or behavioral misconduct with those of the opposite sex and no opportunity to suspect it.

Rule#24

I undertake to abstain from accusing the fellow of teaching the nun for the offering.
This rule helps maintain peace and harmony in the monastery.

Rule#25

I undertake to abstain from giving the robe to the nun.
This rule ensures no opportunity for sexual or behavioral misconduct with those of the opposite sex and no opportunity to suspect it.

Rule#26

I undertake to abstain from sewing the robe for the nun.
This rule ensures no opportunity for sexual or behavioral misconduct with those of the opposite sex and no opportunity to suspect it.

Rule#27

I undertake to abstain from planning a trip with the nun.
This rule ensures no opportunity for sexual or behavioral misconduct with those of the opposite sex and no opportunity to suspect it.

Rule#28

I undertake to abstain from travel by boat with the nun.
This rule ensures no opportunity for sexual or behavioral misconduct with those of the opposite sex and no opportunity to suspect it.

Rule#29

I undertake to abstain from eating the food prepare by the nun.
This rule ensures no opportunity for sexual or behavioral misconduct with those of the opposite sex and no opportunity to suspect it.

Rule#30

I undertake to abstain from sitting in private with the nun.

This rule ensures no opportunity for sexual or behavioral misconduct with those of the opposite sex and no opportunity to suspect it.

Rule#31

I undertake to abstain from eating more than once in a public ceremony.

This rule helps establish self-restraint through proper behavior.

Rule#32

I undertake to abstain from avoiding group meals, except on special occasions such as illness or travel.

This rule keeps the community of monks united.

Rule#33

I undertake to abstain from going to eat another place after eating once.

This rule helps establish self-restraint through proper behavior.

Rule#34

I undertake to abstain from accepting food from more than three bowls.

This rule helps establish self-restraint through proper behavior and prevents greediness.

Rule#35

I undertake to abstain from eating more than once or after mealtime.

This rule helps establish self-restraint through proper behavior and prevents gluttony.

Rule#36

I undertake to abstain from offering the food to the fellow who already ate or after mealtime, later accuse him of misconduct.

This rule helps maintain peace and harmony in the monastery.

Rule#37

I undertake to abstain from eating solid food after midday.

This rule keeps one healthy. Eating two times per day is sufficient for monastic people. It maintains less weight on one's body, which is more comfortable in sitting meditation. Dinner produces energy that may arouse sexual activity at night. Also, there is one less worry about searching for another meal.

Rule#38

I undertake to abstain from eating the food which is kept overnight.

This rule promotes food safety and prevents sickness.

Rule#39

I undertake to abstain from asking for the finest food for oneself.

This rule helps one avoid attachment to worldly desires such as fine food.

Rule#40

I undertake to abstain from eating the food which is not offered by hand.

This rule promotes the idea that nothing should be taken which is not freely given.

Rule#41

I undertake to abstain from giving food by hand to the wanderer.

This rule maintains personal safety from a stranger.

Rule#42

I undertake to abstain from dismissing the fellow after alms round; because I do not want him around.

This rule helps maintain peace and harmony in the monastery.

Rule#43

I undertake to abstain from standing near the house when the couple is in bed.
This rule helps maintain the privacy of the couple in bed. It also prevents monks from sexually arousing.

Rule#44

I undertake to abstain from sitting on the same bench with a woman.
This rule ensures no opportunity for sexual or behavioral misconduct with those of the opposite sex and no opportunity to suspect it.

Rule#45

I undertake to abstain from sitting in private with a woman.
This rule ensures no opportunity for sexual or behavioral misconduct with those of the opposite sex and no opportunity to suspect it.

Rule#46

I undertake to abstain from visiting the laypeople before and after mealtime.
This rule prevents the exploitation of laypeople.

Rule#47

I undertake to abstain from overstocking the health items for more than four months of supplies.

This rule helps maintain detachment to the materials.

Rule#48

I undertake to abstain from watching the military parade.

This rule promotes peacefulness and nonviolence.

Rule#49

I undertake to abstain from spending time with the military for more than three nights.

This rule promotes peacefulness and nonviolence.

Rule#50

I undertake to abstain from watching military activities.

This rule promotes peacefulness and nonviolence.

Rule#51

I undertake to abstain from consuming the intoxicant.

This rule guards one against the dangers of substances that artificially alter the mental and emotional state, taking one out of oneself dangerously and unpredictably.

Rule#52

I undertake to abstain from tickling.
This rule helps establish self-restraint through proper behavior.

Rule#53

I undertake to abstain from playing with water.
This rule helps establish self-restraint through proper behavior.

Rule#54

I undertake to abstain from ignoring the fellow's advice.
This rule keeps one open mind and learns something from others.

Rule#55

I undertake to abstain from frightening the fellow.
This rule helps establish self-restraint through proper behavior.

Rule#56

I undertake to abstain from starting the fire nor ask someone unless I'm sick and need warmth.
This rule promotes safety and necessity.

Rule#57

I undertake to abstain from taking a bath less than twice a month.
This rule maintains health through cleanliness and proper hygiene.

Rule#58

I undertake to abstain from using the robe without a mark on it.
This rule helps avoid conflict for the robe.

Rule#59

I undertake to abstain from exchanging the robe with monk or nun.
This rule helps establish self-restraint through proper behavior.

Rule#60

I undertake to abstain from hiding essential items from fellow.
This rule promotes generosity and compassion among fellows.

Rule#61

I undertake to abstain from killing the animal.
All beings have a right to their lives, and that right should be respected.

Rule#62

I undertake to abstain from using water containing living beings.

All life is sacred and should be treated as such, even the smallest and most insignificant-seeming creatures.

Rule#63

I undertake to abstain from repeating the conflict after the issue was solved.

This rule promotes peace and harmony in the monastery. Conflicts are best to resolve and letting go of them.

Rule#64

I undertake to abstain from concealing the first, second, and third-degree of misconduct.

This rule promotes honest and makes the monk accountable for his actions.

Rule#65

I undertake to abstain from ordaining the under twenty years old person.

This rule promotes the importance of maturity and responsibility.

Rule#66

I undertake to abstain from traveling with the smuggler.

This rule maintains personal safety from a stranger

Rule#67

I undertake to abstain from planning a trip with a woman.
This rule ensures no opportunity for sexual or behavioral misconduct with those of the opposite sex and no opportunity to suspect it.

Rule#68

I undertake to abstain from misrepresenting the teaching.
The teachings are sacred and should always be treated as such.

Rule#69

I undertake to abstain from associating with the fellow who misrepresents the teaching.
The teachings are sacred and should always be treated as such.

Rule#70

I undertake to abstain from staying more than three nights with a fellow who misrepresents the teaching.
The teachings are sacred and should always be treated as such.

Rule#71

I undertake to abstain from skipping a line of the code of conduct.
The teachings are sacred and should always be treated as such.

Rule#72

I undertake to abstain from denying the importance of the code of conduct.
The teachings are sacred and should always be treated as such.

Rule#73

I undertake to abstain from ignoring the code of conduct.
The teachings are sacred and should always be treated as such.

Rule#74

I undertake to abstain from hitting the fellow.
This rule promotes peacefulness and nonviolence among monks.

Rule#75

I undertake to abstain from threatening the fellow with a gesture.
This rule promotes peacefulness and nonviolence among monks.

Rule#76

I undertake to abstain from accusing the fellow with second-degree misconduct without clear evidence.

This rule helps maintain peace and harmony in the monastery.

Rule#77

I undertake to abstain from provoking stress or anxiety to the fellow.

This rule helps maintain peace and harmony in the monastery.

Rule#78

I undertake to abstain from listening to the argument.

This rule helps maintain peace and harmony in the monastery.

Rule#79

I undertake to abstain from flip-flopping.

This rule helps maintain peace and harmony in the monastery.

Rule#80

I undertake to abstain from skipping the administration meeting.

This rule maintains the importance of the proper functioning of the monastery and should be attended.

Rule#81

I undertake to abstain from criticizing the administrator who distributes the robe.
This rule maintains the importance of the proper functioning of the monastery and should be respected.

Rule#82

I undertake to abstain from diverting the gift for the fellow to other people.
This rule promotes honesty among fellows.

Rule#83

I undertake to abstain from meeting the King and the Queen in the chamber(bedroom).
This rule prevents overindulgence in sensual pleasure.

Rule#84

I undertake to abstain from picking up the valuable items outside the monastery nor ask someone.
This rule prevents attachment to materials.

Rule#85

I undertake to abstain from entering the town or village without notifying the fellow.
This rule maintains the personal safety of fellows by alerting others to one's whereabouts.

Rule#86

I undertake to abstain from using a sewing kit made of ivory, bone, or horn.

This rule prevents attachment to materials made from the animal part.

Rule#87

I undertake to abstain from using a chair or bed of a height greater than 65 cm.

This rule promotes safety and maintains humility.

Rule#88

I undertake to abstain from using the cotton cushion.

This rule promotes humility and prevents attachment to materials.

Rule#89

I undertake to abstain from sitting on clothes bigger than 2.20mx1.72m with a corner over 35cm of width.

This rule promotes humility and prevents attachment to materials.

Rule#90

I undertake to abstain from using the robe as the bandage larger than 4.5mx2.20m.

This rule promotes modesty.

Rule#91

I undertake to abstain from using a rain robe bigger than 6.5mx2.70m.

This rule promotes modesty.

Rule#92

I undertake to abstain from using a robe bigger than 10mx6.5m.

This rule promotes modesty.

Sixth-degree misconduct

Rule#1

I undertake to abstain from accepting food from the nun.

This rule ensures no opportunity for sexual or behavioral misconduct with those of the opposite sex and no opportunity to suspect it.

Rule#2

I undertake to abstain from allowing the nun to serve the food during mealtime.

This rule ensures no opportunity for sexual or behavioral misconduct with those of the opposite sex and no opportunity to suspect it.

Rule#3

I undertake to abstain from receiving food from the poor without the invitation.

This rule prevents the exploitation of the poor.

Rule#4

I undertake to abstain from eating the food in a dangerous area.

This rule promotes personal safety.

Seventh-degree misconduct

Rule#1

I undertake to wear the lower robe properly.
This rule keeps one looking proper and humble.

Rule#2

I undertake to wear the upper robe properly.
This rule keeps one looking proper and humble.

Rule#3

I undertake to close the robe up to the neck and down to the wrist when sitting in public.
This rule keeps one looking proper and humble.

Rule#4

I undertake to close the robe up to the neck and down to the wrist when walking in public.
This rule keeps one looking proper and humble.

Rule#5

I undertake to be well restrained when sitting in public.
This rule helps one maintain his composure with proper behavior.

Rule#6

I undertake to be well restrained when walking in public.

This rule avoids unnecessary movements and maintains a sense of discipline, mindfulness, and focus.

Rule#7

I undertake to keep the eyes low when sitting in public.

This rule helps prevent the eyes from wandering.

Rule#8

I undertake to keep the eyes low when walking in public.

This rule helps prevent the eyes from wandering.

Rule#9

I undertake to abstain from lifting the robe when sitting in public.

This rule preserves modesty.

Rule#10

I undertake to abstain from lifting the robe when walking in public.

This rule preserves modesty.

Rule#11

I undertake to abstain from laughing too loud when sitting in public.

This rule reminds one to remain calm and mindful in public instead of being overexcited.

Rule#12

I undertake to abstain from laughing too loud when walking in public.

This rule reminds one to remain calm and mindful in public instead of being overexcited.

Rule#13

I undertake to abstain from speaking too loudly when sitting in public.

This rule reminds one to remain calm and mindful in public.

Rule#14

I undertake to abstain from speaking too loudly when walking in public.

This rule reminds one to remain calm and mindful in public.

Rule#15

I undertake to abstain from swinging the body when sitting in public.

This rule helps one maintain his composure with proper behavior.

Rule#16

I undertake to abstain from swinging the body when walking in public.
This rule avoids unnecessary movements and maintains a sense of discipline, mindfulness, and focus.

Rule#17

I undertake to abstain from swinging the arm when sitting in public.
This rule helps one maintain his composure with proper behavior.

Rule#18

I undertake to abstain from swinging the arm when walking in public.
This rule avoids unnecessary movements and maintains a sense of discipline, mindfulness, and focus.

Rule#19

I undertake to abstain from shaking the head when sitting in public.
This rule helps one maintain his composure with proper behavior.

Rule#20

I undertake to abstain from shaking the head when walking in public.

This rule avoids unnecessary movements maintains a sense of discipline, mindfulness, and focus.

Rule#21

I undertake to abstain from placing the hand on the hip when sitting in public.

This rule helps one to avoid an arrogant appearance.

Rule#22

I undertake to abstain from placing the hand on the hip when walking in public.

This rule helps one to avoid an arrogant appearance.

Rule#23

I undertake to abstain from covering the head when sitting in public.

This rule helps one to maintain a proper and honest appearance.

Rule#24

I undertake to abstain from covering the head when walking in public.

This rule helps one to maintain a proper and honest appearance.

Rule#25

I undertake to abstain from standing on tiptoes or the heels in public.
This rule helps one maintain his composure with proper behavior.

Rule#26

I undertake to abstain from sitting with the knees raised and the arms wrapped around the legs when in public.
This rule helps one maintain his composure with proper behavior.

Rule#27

I undertake to be respectful when receiving alms-food.
This rule reminds one to always being mindful of receiving food with appreciation and respect.

Rule#28

I undertake to keep attention on the bowl when receiving alms-food.
This rule reminds one to always being mindful of eating food with appreciation and respect.

Rule#29

I undertake to receive alms-food in proportion (for example, one part of curry, three rice parts).
This rule reminds one of always receiving food in proportion and being humble.

Rule#30

I undertake to receive alms-food without exceeding the inner trim.

This rule reminds one of always being mindful of receiving food with appreciation and respect instead of greediness.

Rule#31

I undertake to be well restrained when eating.

This rule reminds one to always being mindful of eating food with appreciation and respect.

Rule#32

I undertake to keep attention on the bowl when eating.

This rule reminds one to always being mindful of eating food with appreciation and respect.

Rule#33

I undertake to eat the food in order, not picky.

This rule reminds one to always being mindful of eating food properly.

Rule#34

I undertake to eat food in proportion (for example, one spoon of curry, three rice spoons).

This rule reminds one of always eating in proportion and being humble.

Rule#35

I undertake to abstain from eating from the top of a heap of food. I take food from a site.

This rule reminds one to be well-restrained in eating.

Rule#36

I undertake to abstain from hiding tasty food in order the get more.

This rule reminds one of always being mindful of eating food with appreciation and respect instead of greediness.

Rule#37

I undertake to abstain from asking for food if not sick.

This rule reminds one to abstain from being too lazy to go out for alms-food.

Rule#38

I undertake to abstain from looking at the fellow bowl with jealousy.

This rule reminds one to appreciate the food he has and refrain from falling into the trap of greed and desire.

Rule#39

I undertake to abstain from making a large lump of food.

This rule reminds one to be well-restrained in eating.

Rule#40

I undertake to make a lump of food suitable for a mouthful.

This rule reminds one to be well-restrained in eating.

Rule#41

I undertake to abstain from opening the mouth before the food arrives at the mouth.

This rule reminds one to be well-restrained in eating.

Rule#42

I undertake to abstain from putting the finger into the mouth.

This rule helps one maintain his composure with proper behavior.

Rule#43

I undertake to abstain from speaking while eating food.

This rule promotes respect and self-restraint through proper behavior.

Rule#44

I undertake to abstain from throwing the food into the mouth.

This rule promotes respect and self-restraint through proper behavior.

Rule#45

I undertake to abstain from biting off the food.
This rule promotes respect and self-restraint through proper behavior.

Rule#46

I undertake to abstain from stuffing out the cheeks with food.
This rule promotes respect and self-restraint through proper behavior.

Rule#47

I undertake to abstain from shaking off the food.
This rule promotes respect and self-restraint through proper behavior.

Rule#48

I undertake to abstain from scattering the food.
This rule promotes respect and self-restraint through proper behavior.

Rule#49

I undertake to abstain from letting the tongue out.
This rule promotes respect and self-restraint through proper behavior.

Rule#50

I undertake to abstain from making champing noise when eating.

This rule promotes respect and self-restraint through proper behavior.

Rule#51

I undertake to abstain from making a sucking noise when dinking.

This rule promotes respect and self-restraint through proper behavior.

Rule#52

I undertake to abstain from licking the hand.

This rule promotes respect and self-restraint through proper behavior.

Rule#53

I undertake to abstain from scraping the bowl.

This rule promotes respect and self-restraint through proper behavior.

Rule#54

I undertake to abstain from licking the lips.

This rule promotes respect and self-restraint through proper behavior.

Rule#55

I undertake to abstain from washing hands, which still had the food.

This rule helps one to be well-restrained after eating and to avoid wasting food.

Rule#56

I undertake to abstain from throw out bowl-washing water, which still had the food.

This rule helps one to be well-restrained after eating and to avoid wasting food.

Rule#57

I undertake to abstain from teaching the person holding the umbrella.

This rule maintains personal safety from a stranger.

Rule#58

I undertake to abstain from teaching the person holding the walking stick.

This rule maintains personal safety from a stranger.

Rule#59

I undertake to abstain from teaching the person holding the sharp tool.

This rule maintains personal safety from a stranger.

Rule#60

I undertake to abstain from teaching the person holding the weapon.

This rule maintains personal safety from a stranger.

Rule#61

I undertake to abstain from teaching the person wearing shoes.

This rule maintains the value of teaching. The instructor requires attention and respect from the listener.

Rule#62

I undertake to abstain from teaching the person wearing sandals.

This rule maintains the value of teaching. The instructor requires attention and respect from the listener.

Rule#63

I undertake to abstain from teaching the person in the vehicle.

This rule maintains the value of teaching. The instructor requires attention and respect from the listener.

Rule#64

I undertake to abstain from teaching the person who is lying down.

This rule maintains the value of teaching. The instructor requires attention and respect from the listener.

Rule#65

I undertake to abstain from teaching the person sitting with the knees raised and the arms wrapped around the legs.

This rule maintains the value of teaching. The instructor requires attention and respect from the listener.

Rule#66

I undertake to abstain from teaching the person wearing a hat.

This rule maintains the value of teaching. The instructor requires attention and respect from the listener.

Rule#67

I undertake to abstain from teaching the person wearing the scarf to cover the head.

This rule maintains the value of teaching. The instructor requires attention and respect from the listener.

Rule#68

I undertake to abstain from teaching the person sitting on the seat while I'm sitting on the ground.

This rule maintains the value of teaching. The instructor requires attention and respect from the listener.

Rule#69

I undertake to abstain from teaching the person sitting on the high chair while I'm sitting on a lower chair.

This rule maintains the value of teaching. The instructor requires attention and respect from the listener.

Rule#70

I undertake to abstain from teaching the person who is sitting while I'm standing.

This rule maintains the value of teaching. The instructor requires attention and respect from the listener.

Rule#71

I undertake to abstain from teaching the person who is walking ahead.

This rule maintains the value of teaching. The instructor requires attention and respect from the listener.

Rule#72

I undertake to abstain from teaching the person walking on the pathway while I walk on the sideway.

This rule maintains the value of teaching. The instructor requires attention and respect from the listener.

Rule#73

I undertake to abstain from defecating or urinating while standing.

This rule preserves modesty.

Rule#74

I undertake to abstain from defecating or urinating, or spitting on the living plants.

All life is sacred, including plants. They, therefore, deserve to be respected.

Rule#75

I undertake to abstain from defecating or urinating, or spitting into the water.

This rule prevents one from contaminating water fit for drinking or bathing. Not only does it promote good hygiene and healthy living, but it is also a matter of respect.

The verdict

1. **The administrator should give the verdict face to face.**

This rule promotes honest verdicts and makes the monk accountable for his actions.

2. **If the monk is innocent, the verdict should be "mindfulness."**

Mindfulness is a way of life for those in the monastic community and should always be adopted.

3. **If the monk was out of mind when he committed the offense, the verdict should be "past insanity."**

This rule protects monks who are temporarily insane.

4. **If the monk confesses to the offense, the verdict should be "following what was admitted."**

Confessing to a crime is a form of honesty, which is promoted in monastic life.

5. **In some cases, the majority vote of administrators can decide on the case.**

Using a majority vote of administrators to poll all those involved is a valuable tool, especially in cases that influence everyone.

6. **If the monk confesses after interrogation, the verdict should go further.**

Despite the honesty of a confession, interrogations should be pursued to determine an account of what happened and how it should be dealt with.

7. **If both monks settled the dispute and admitted the mistakes. The administrator should give the verdict, "covering over as with grass."**

At this point, the dispute has been handled, and the decision should be met with respect.

Rules for the nun
Four precepts for the nun

1. I'm well restrained to the rules of conduct.

Monastic life requires its members to both practices good, helpful acts and avoid bad behavior to live purely and focus on the path to Enlightenment. This involves strictly adhering to a set of rules that promote a life that is humble, proper, respectful, and mindful.

2. I restrain my eyes, ears, nose, mouth, body, and emotion.

From her body to her mind, every part of the nun should maintain focus on her path. This means that no part of herself should create or give into desires or feelings of hatred.

3. I live with the right livelihood.

Nuns are expected to live wholesome lives in which they perform only good acts and are respectful at all times of all life and mindful of the rules set out for them. This includes regarding all life as sacred, harming no being, speaking only the truth, and refraining from misleading or seducing others.

4. **I contemplate the four offerings (food, medicine, robe, and shelter).**

Nuns are expected to contemplate the four offerings, which are the necessities required for basic life. In this contemplation, they should refrain from attachment and desire while mindfully respecting and appreciating the offerings that keep them alive and allow them the freedom to follow their path with their basic needs met.

Additional 227 rules for the nun
First-degree misconduct

Rule#1

I undertake to abstain from sexual contact with humans or animals.

Sexuality is a powerful force, one that is easy to get pulled into. Nuns need to remain chaste to focus their energy on their path and resist the pull of desire.

Rule#2

I undertake to abstain from stealing.

The mindful and moral life of nuns includes being careful in their dealings with others only to take theirs and are freely given.

Rule#3

I undertake to abstain from killing a human.

Human life is sacred. It is no one's place to judge another life or decide who gets to live or die.

Rule#4

I undertake to abstain from the false claim of high attainment achievement.

Words are powerful to ourselves and others, creating the course of our lives and relationships. Truth is precious and should be adhered to at all times.

Second-degree misconduct

Rule#1

I undertake to abstain from masturbation.
This rule helps nuns stay calm and mindful instead of forming attachments to the physical world and getting lost in desire.

Rule#2

I undertake to abstain from physically contacting the man with lust.
Sexuality is a powerful force, one that is easy to get pulled into. Nuns need to remain chaste and virtuous so they can focus their energy on their path and resist the pull of desire. This includes abstaining from any act that leads one to think of or desire to engage in sexual thoughts or acts.

Rule#3

I undertake to abstain from flirting with a man.
Though flirting might seem like an innocent act, it is the first step that leads to sexual thoughts and activity. This rule helps nuns maintain a virtuous mind.

Rule#4

I undertake to abstain from seducing a man for sex.
This rule helps maintain chastity and avoids any potential for or suspicions of misconduct, beyond a doubt, with those of the opposite sex.

Rule#5

I undertake to abstain from engaging the man with a woman.

This rule helps avoid arranging the marriage.

Rule#6

I undertake to abstain from asking someone to make a shelter larger than (3m x 1.75m) for me without administrator approval.

This rule helps avoid attachment to the materials and exploiting the laypeople.

Rule#7

I undertake to abstain from asking someone to make a building for me without administrator approval.

This rule helps avoid attachment to the materials and exploiting the laypeople.

Rule#8

I undertake to abstain from accusing the fellow of serious misconduct without clear evidence.

This rule helps maintain peace and harmony in the monastery.

Rule#9

I undertake to abstain from accusing the fellow of serious misconduct with exaggerated false claims.
This rule helps maintain peace and harmony in the monastery.

Rule#10

I undertake to abstain from creating a division in the monastery.
This rule helps maintain peace and harmony in the monastery.

Rule#11

I undertake to abstain from participating with others to create a division in the monastery.
This rule helps maintain peace and harmony in the monastery.

Rule#12

I undertake to abstain from defying the judgment of the administrator.
This rule helps maintain a level of respect and order within the monastery.

Rule#13

I undertake to abstain from exploiting the laypeople.
This rule helps gain trust and respect from laypeople.

Third-degree misconduct

Rule#1

I undertake to abstain from being in private with a man, which creates doubt of sexual contact.
This rule helps maintain chastity and avoids any potential for or suspicions of misconduct, beyond doubt, with those of the opposite sex.

Rule#2

I undertake to abstain from being in private with a man, which creates doubt of flirting.
Though flirting might seem like an innocent act, it is the first step that leads to sexual thoughts and activity. This rule helps nuns maintain a virtuous mind.

Fourth-degree misconduct

Rule#1

I undertake to abstain from keeping the extra robes for more than ten days. (3 robes are permitted)
This rule helps avoid attachment to the materials.

Rule#2

I undertake to abstain from sleeping far from the robes.
This rule helps prevent misplacing one's robes.

Rule#3

I undertake to abstain from keeping cloth to make new robe than one month.
This rule helps avoid attachment to the materials.

Rule#4

I undertake to abstain from asking a non-relative monk to wash or dye the robe.
This rule keeps one from improper contact with the opposite sex.

Rule#5

I undertake to abstain from receiving the robe from the non-relative monk.
This rule keeps one from improper contact with the opposite sex.

Rule#6

I undertake to abstain from asking non-relative lay-people for a robe.

This rule prevents the exploitation of laypeople.

Rule#7

I undertake to abstain from asking for more than one set of the robe in case of losing all the three robes.

This rule prevents the exploitation of laypeople.

Rule#8

I undertake to abstain from asking laypeople for the finest robe.

This rule prevents the exploitation of laypeople.

Rule#9

I undertake to abstain from asking another layperson of an extra finest robe.

This rule prevents the exploitation of laypeople.

Rule#10

I undertake to abstain from asking the assistance (the money keeper) for an essential item more than three times, not stand in front of him more than six times. If I do not get the item, I inform the donor to get their money back from the assistance.

This rule keeps everyone honest and accountable.

Rule#11

I undertake to abstain from accepting the silk carpet.
This rule helps avoid attachment to the materials.

Rule#12

I undertake to abstain from accepting the carpet made of 100percent black sheep wool.
This rule helps avoid attachment to the materials.

Rule#13

I undertake to abstain from accepting the carpet made of black sheep wool and the white sheep wool.
This rule helps avoid attachment to the materials.

Rule#14

I undertake to abstain from accepting the new carpet unless the old one is over six years old.
This rule helps avoid attachment to the materials.

Rule#15

I undertake to abstain from using the new carpet without some part of the old one.
This rule helps avoid attachment to the materials.

Rule#16

I undertake to abstain from carrying the raw wool for more than three walking days (48km).
This rule avoids attachment to the materials.

Rule#17

I undertake to abstain from asking the monk or nun to wash, dye the wool.

This rule prevents the exploitation of the fellow.

Rule#18

I undertake to abstain from accepting the money.

Those in the monastic community have their basic needs met. Therefore, they need no money.

Rule#19

I undertake to abstain from handling the money.

Those in the monastic community have their basic needs met. Therefore, they need no money.

Rule#20

I undertake to abstain from exchange things.

Those in the monastic community have their basic needs met.

Rule#21

I undertake to abstain from keeping an extra bowl (food container) for more than ten days.

This rule helps those in the monastic community avoid attachment to the materials.

Rule#22

I undertake to abstain from asking for a new bowl (food container) unless the old one was broken or unusable.
This rule helps those in the monastic community avoid attachment to the materials.

Rule#23

I undertake to abstain from keeping the food as medicine for more than seven days.
This rule promotes healthy living through proper food usage.

Rule#24

I undertake to abstain from receiving the rain robe long before the rainy retreat season.
This rule promotes humility and prevents attachment to materials.

Rule#25

I undertake to abstain from taking back the robe after giving it away.
This rule keeps everyone honest and accountable.

Rule#26

I undertake to abstain from making the finest robe for myself.
This rule helps those in the monastic community avoid attachment to the materials.

Rule#27

I undertake to abstain from ordering the finest robe.
This rule helps those in the monastic community avoid attachment to the materials.

Rule#28

I undertake to abstain from accepting the extra robe unless authorized.
This rule helps those in the monastic community avoid attachment to the materials.

Rule#29

I undertake to abstain from leaving the robe for more than six nights. (except the rainy retreat season).
This rule prevents one from losing the robe.

Rule#30

I undertake to abstain from diverting the donation to myself if it's intended for all the fellow.
This rule keeps everyone honest and accountable.

Fifth-degree misconduct

Rule#1

I undertake to abstain from lying.
This rule helps nuns preserve the sanctity of truth while also keeping them virtuous.

Rule#2

I undertake to abstain from insulting another fellow.
This rule helps maintain peace among fellow and reminds one to treat others with kindness.

Rule#3

I undertake to abstain from arguing with another fellow.
This rule helps maintain peace among fellow and reminds one to treat others with kindness.

Rule#4

I undertake to abstain from reciting the text with the laypeople.
The nunhood is sacred. This rule helps maintain its sanctity.

Rule#5

I undertake to abstain from sleeping in the same building with laypeople for more than three nights.
This rule prevents laypeople's exploitation and ensures that nuns realize that their home is in the monastery instead of out in the world with laypeople.

Rule#6

I undertake to abstain from lying down in the building where the man is also there.

This rule ensures no opportunity for sexual or behavioral misconduct with those of the opposite sex and no opportunity to suspect it.

Rule#7

I undertake to abstain from teaching the man without the presence of another woman.

This rule ensures no opportunity for sexual or behavioral misconduct with those of the opposite sex and no opportunity to suspect it.

Rule#8

I undertake to abstain from telling the achievement of attainment to laypeople.

This rule helps maintain humility and avoid bragging.

Rule#9

I undertake to abstain from revealing the severe misconduct of the fellow to the laypeople.

This rule protects the fellows and the monastery as a whole from outside suspicion and trouble. People, including nuns, will always make mistakes, but they can learn from them and grow not to commit the offense again. There is no need to involved the outside community in the inner affairs of the monastery.

Rule#10

I undertake to abstain from digging the ground or ask someone to do it.

This rule is a reminder that all life is sacred and should be treated as such, including plants and small creatures.

Rule#11

I undertake to abstain from damaging the living plants.

This rule is a reminder that all life is sacred and should be treated as such, including plants.

Rule#12

I undertake to abstain from finding the fault of the administrator.

This rule helps maintain a level of respect and order within the monastery.

Rule#13

I undertake to abstain from criticizing the fellow.

This rule helps maintain peace and harmony in the monastery.

Rule#14

I undertake to abstain from using a chair or bed in public, then leave without returning it to a proper place.

This rule helps keep the public in proper order.

Rule#15

I undertake to abstain from using a chair or bed in the monastery, then leave without returning it to a proper place.

This rule helps keep the monastery in proper order.

Rule#16

I undertake to abstain from intruding the occupied dwelling.

This rule helps maintain peace and harmony in the monastery.

Rule#17

I undertake to abstain from expelling the roommate from the dwelling.

This rule is a reminder for nuns to be kind and thoughtful to their fellows.

Rule#18

I undertake to abstain from using the bed or chair, which is not ready for use.

This rule keeps everyone safe from injury.

Rule#19

I undertake to abstain from building a roof with more than three layers.

This rule keeps everyone safe from injury.

Rule#20

I undertake to abstain from pouring the water containing the insect.

All life is sacred and should be treated as such, even the smallest creatures such as insects.

Rule#21

I undertake to abstain from teaching the monk without the approval of the administrator.

This rule ensures no opportunity for sexual or behavioral misconduct with those of the opposite sex and no opportunity to suspect it.

Rule#22

I undertake to abstain from teaching the monk after sunset.

This rule ensures no opportunity for sexual or behavioral misconduct with those of the opposite sex and no opportunity to suspect it.

Rule#23

I undertake to abstain from going to the monk dwelling for teaching.

This rule ensures no opportunity for sexual or behavioral misconduct with those of the opposite sex and no opportunity to suspect it.

Rule#24

I undertake to abstain from accusing the fellow of teaching the monks for the offering.
This rule helps maintain peace and harmony in the monastery.

Rule#25

I undertake to abstain from giving the robe to the monk.
This rule ensures no opportunity for sexual or behavioral misconduct with those of the opposite sex and no opportunity to suspect it.

Rule#26

I undertake to abstain from sewing the robe for the monk.
This rule ensures no opportunity for sexual or behavioral misconduct with those of the opposite sex and no opportunity to suspect it.

Rule#27

I undertake to abstain from planning a trip with the monk.
This rule ensures no opportunity for sexual or behavioral misconduct with those of the opposite sex and no opportunity to suspect it.

Rule#28

I undertake to abstain from travel by boat with the monk.

This rule ensures no opportunity for sexual or behavioral misconduct with those of the opposite sex and no opportunity to suspect it.

Rule#29

I undertake to abstain from eating the food prepare by the monk.

This rule ensures no opportunity for sexual or behavioral misconduct with those of the opposite sex and no opportunity to suspect it.

Rule#30

I undertake to abstain from sitting in private with the monk.

This rule ensures no opportunity for sexual or behavioral misconduct with those of the opposite sex and no opportunity to suspect it.

Rule#31

I undertake to abstain from eating more than once in a public ceremony.

This rule helps establish self-restraint through proper behavior.

Rule#32

I undertake to abstain from avoiding group meals, except on special occasions such as illness or travel.
This rule keeps the community of nuns united.

Rule#33

I undertake to abstain from going to eat another place after eating once.
This rule helps establish self-restraint through proper behavior.

Rule#34

I undertake to abstain from accepting food from more than three bowls.
This rule helps establish self-restraint through proper behavior and prevents greediness.

Rule#35

I undertake to abstain from eating more than once or after mealtime.
This rule helps establish self-restraint through proper behavior and prevents gluttony.

Rule#36

I undertake to abstain from offering the food to the fellow who already ate or after mealtime, later accuse him of misconduct.

This rule helps maintain peace and harmony in the monastery.

Rule#37

I undertake to abstain from eating solid food after midday.

This rule keeps one healthy. Eating two times per day is sufficient for monastic people. It maintains less weight on one's body, which is more comfortable in sitting meditation. Dinner produces energy that may arouse sexual activity at night. Also, there is one less worry about searching for another meal.

Rule#38

I undertake to abstain from eating the food which is kept overnight.

This rule promotes food safety and prevents sickness.

Rule#39

I undertake to abstain from asking for the finest food for oneself.

This rule helps one avoid attachment to worldly desires such as fine food.

Rule#40

I undertake to abstain from eating the food which is not offered by hand.

This rule promotes the idea that nothing should be taken which is not freely given.

Rule#41

I undertake to abstain from giving food by hand to the wanderer.

This rule maintains personal safety from a stranger.

Rule#42

I undertake to abstain from dismissing the fellow after alms round; because I do not want him around.

This rule helps maintain peace and harmony in the monastery.

Rule#43

I undertake to abstain from standing near the house when the couple is in bed.

This rule helps maintain the privacy of the couple in bed. It also prevents nuns from sexually arousing.

Rule#44

I undertake to abstain from sitting on the same bench with a man.

This rule ensures no opportunity for sexual or behavioral misconduct with those of the opposite sex and no opportunity to suspect it.

Rule#45

I undertake to abstain from sitting in private with a man.

This rule ensures no opportunity for sexual or behavioral misconduct with those of the opposite sex and no opportunity to suspect it.

Rule#46

I undertake to abstain from visiting the laypeople before and after mealtime.

This rule prevents the exploitation of laypeople.

Rule#47

I undertake to abstain from overstocking the health items for more than four months of supplies.

This rule helps maintain detachment to the materials.

Rule#48

I undertake to abstain from watching the military parade.

This rule promotes peacefulness and nonviolence.

Rule#49

I undertake to abstain from spending time with the military for more than three nights.

This rule promotes peacefulness and nonviolence.

Rule#50

I undertake to abstain from watching military activities.

This rule promotes peacefulness and nonviolence.

Rule#51

I undertake to abstain from consuming the intoxicant.

This rule guards one against the dangers of substances that artificially alter the mental and emotional state, taking one out of oneself dangerously and unpredictably.

Rule#52

I undertake to abstain from tickling.

This rule helps establish self-restraint through proper behavior.

Rule#53

I undertake to abstain from playing with water.

This rule helps establish self-restraint through proper behavior.

Rule#54

I undertake to abstain from ignoring the fellow's advice.
This rule keeps one open mind and learns something from others.

Rule#55

I undertake to abstain from frightening the fellow.
This rule helps establish self-restraint through proper behavior.

Rule#56

I undertake to abstain from starting the fire nor ask someone unless I'm sick and need warmth.
This rule promotes safety and necessity.

Rule#57

I undertake to abstain from taking a bath less than twice a month.
This rule maintains health through cleanliness and proper hygiene.

Rule#58

I undertake to abstain from using the robe without a mark on it.
Thie rule helps avoid conflict for the robe.

Rule#59

I undertake to abstain from exchanging the robe with monk or nun.

This rule helps establish self-restraint through proper behavior.

Rule#60

I undertake to abstain from hiding essential items from fellow.

This rule promotes generosity and compassion among fellows.

Rule#61

I undertake to abstain from killing the animal.

All beings have a right to their lives, and that right should be respected.

Rule#62

I undertake to abstain from using water containing living beings.

All life is sacred and should be treated as such, even the smallest and most insignificant-seeming creatures.

Rule#63

I undertake to abstain from repeating the conflict after the issue was solved.

This rule promotes peace and harmony in the monastery. Conflicts are best to resolve and letting go of them.

Rule#64

I undertake to abstain from concealing the first, second, and third-degree of misconduct.
This rule promotes honest and makes the nun accountable for her actions.

Rule#65

I undertake to abstain from ordaining the under twenty years old person.
This rule promotes the importance of maturity and responsibility.

Rule#66

I undertake to abstain from traveling with the smuggler.
This rule maintains personal safety from a stranger

Rule#67

I undertake to abstain from planning a trip with a man.
This rule ensures no opportunity for sexual or behavioral misconduct with those of the opposite sex and no opportunity to suspect it.

Rule#68

I undertake to abstain from misrepresenting the teaching.
The teachings are sacred and should always be treated as such.

Rule#69

I undertake to abstain from associating with the fellow who misrepresents the teaching.
The teachings are sacred and should always be treated as such.

Rule#70

I undertake to abstain from staying more than three nights with a fellow who misrepresents the teaching.
The teachings are sacred and should always be treated as such.

Rule#71

I undertake to abstain from skipping a line of the code of conduct.
The teachings are sacred and should always be treated as such.

Rule#72

I undertake to abstain from denying the importance of the code of conduct.
The teachings are sacred and should always be treated as such.

Rule#73

I undertake to abstain from ignoring the code of conduct.
The teachings are sacred and should always be treated as such.

Rule#74

I undertake to abstain from hitting the fellow.
This rule promotes peacefulness and nonviolence among nuns.

Rule#75

I undertake to abstain from threatening the fellow with a gesture.
This rule promotes peacefulness and nonviolence among nuns.

Rule#76

I undertake to abstain from accusing the fellow with second-degree misconduct without clear evidence.
This rule helps maintain peace and harmony in the monastery.

Rule#77

I undertake to abstain from provoking stress or anxiety to the fellow.
This rule helps maintain peace and harmony in the monastery.

Rule#78

I undertake to abstain from listening to the argument.
This rule helps maintain peace and harmony in the monastery.

Rule#79

I undertake to abstain from flip-flopping.
This rule promotes honesty among fellows.

Rule#80

I undertake to abstain from skipping the administration meeting.
This rule maintains the importance of the proper functioning of the monastery and should be attended.

Rule#81

I undertake to abstain from criticizing the administrator who distributes the robe.
This rule maintains the importance of the proper functioning of the monastery and should be respected.

Rule#82

I undertake to abstain from diverting the gift for the fellow to other people.
This rule promotes honesty among fellows.

Rule#83

I undertake to abstain from meeting the King and the Queen in the chamber(bedroom).

This rule prevents overindulgence in sensual pleasure.

Rule#84

I undertake to abstain from picking up the valuable items outside the monastery nor ask someone.

This rule prevents attachment to materials.

Rule#85

I undertake to abstain from entering the town or village without notifying the fellow.

This rule maintains the personal safety of fellows by alerting others to one's whereabouts.

Rule#86

I undertake to abstain from using a sewing kit made of ivory, bone, or horn.

This rule prevents attachment to materials made from the animal part.

Rule#87

I undertake to abstain from using a chair or bed of a height greater than 65 cm.

This rule promotes safety and maintains humility.

Rule#88

I undertake to abstain from using the cotton cushion.
This rule promotes humility and prevents attachment to materials.

Rule#89

I undertake to abstain from sitting on clothes bigger than 2.20mx1.72m with a corner over 35cm of width.
This rule promotes humility and prevents attachment to materials.

Rule#90

I undertake to abstain from using the robe as the bandage larger than 4.5mx2.20m.
This rule promotes modesty.

Rule#91

I undertake to abstain from using a rain robe bigger than 6.5mx2.70m.
This rule promotes modesty.

Rule#92

I undertake to abstain from using a robe bigger than 10mx6.5m.
This rule promotes modesty.

Sixth-degree misconduct

Rule#1

I undertake to abstain from accepting food from the monk.

This rule ensures no opportunity for sexual or behavioral misconduct with those of the opposite sex and no opportunity to suspect it.

Rule#2

I undertake to abstain from allowing the monk to serve the food during mealtime.

This rule ensures no opportunity for sexual or behavioral misconduct with those of the opposite sex and no opportunity to suspect it.

Rule#3

I undertake to abstain from receiving food from the poor without the invitation.

This rule prevents the exploitation of the poor.

Rule#4

I undertake to abstain from eating the food in a dangerous area.

This rule promotes personal safety.

Seventh-degree misconduct

Rule#1

I undertake to wear the lower robe properly.
This rule keeps one looking proper and humble.

Rule#2

I undertake to wear the upper robe properly.
This rule keeps one looking proper and humble.

Rule#3

I undertake to close the robe up to the neck and down to the wrist when sitting in public.
This rule keeps one looking proper and humble.

Rule#4

I undertake to close the robe up to the neck and down to the wrist when walking in public.
This rule keeps one looking proper and humble.

Rule#5

I undertake to be well restrained when sitting in public.
This rule helps one maintain her composure with proper behavior.

Rule#6

I undertake to be well restrained when walking in public.

This rule avoids unnecessary movements and maintains a sense of discipline, mindfulness, and focus.

Rule#7

I undertake to keep the eyes low when sitting in public.

This rule helps prevent the eyes from wandering.

Rule#8

I undertake to keep the eyes low when walking in public.

This rule helps prevent the eyes from wandering.

Rule#9

I undertake to abstain from lifting the robe when sitting in public.

This rule preserves modesty.

Rule#10

I undertake to abstain from lifting the robe when walking in public.

This rule preserves modesty.

Rule#11

I undertake to abstain from laughing too loud when sitting in public.

This rule reminds one to remain calm and mindful in public instead of being overexcited.

Rule#12

I undertake to abstain from laughing too loud when walking in public.

This rule reminds one to remain calm and mindful in public instead of being overexcited.

Rule#13

I undertake to abstain from speaking too loudly when sitting in public.

This rule reminds one to remain calm and mindful in public.

Rule#14

I undertake to abstain from speaking too loudly when walking in public.

This rule reminds one to remain calm and mindful in public.

Rule#15

I undertake to abstain from swinging the body when sitting in public.

This rule helps one maintain her composure with proper behavior.

Rule#16

I undertake to abstain from swinging the body when walking in public.

This rule avoids unnecessary movements and maintains a sense of discipline, mindfulness, and focus.

Rule#17

I undertake to abstain from swinging the arm when sitting in public.

This rule helps one maintain her composure with proper behavior.

Rule#18

I undertake to abstain from swinging the arm when walking in public.

This rule avoids unnecessary movements and maintains a sense of discipline, mindfulness, and focus.

Rule#19

I undertake to abstain from shaking the head when sitting in public.

This rule helps one maintain her composure with proper behavior.

Rule#20

I undertake to abstain from shaking the head when walking in public.

This rule avoids unnecessary movements and maintains a sense of discipline, mindfulness, and focus.

Rule#21

I undertake to abstain from placing the hand on the hip when sitting in public.

This rule helps one to avoid an arrogant appearance.

Rule#22

I undertake to abstain from placing the hand on the hip when walking in public.

This rule helps one to avoid an arrogant appearance.

Rule#23

I undertake to abstain from covering the head when sitting in public.

This rule helps one to maintain a proper and honest appearance.

Rule#24

I undertake to abstain from covering the head when walking in public.

This rule helps one to maintain a proper and honest appearance.

Rule#25

I undertake to abstain from standing on tiptoes or the heels in public.

This rule helps one maintain her composure with proper behavior.

Rule#26

I undertake to abstain from sitting with the knees raised and the arms wrapped around the legs when in public.

This rule helps one maintain her composure with proper behavior.

Rule#27

I undertake to be respectful when receiving alms-food.

This rule reminds one to always being mindful of receiving food with appreciation and respect.

Rule#28

I undertake to keep attention on the bowl when receiving alms-food.

This rule reminds one to always being mindful of receiving food with appreciation and respect.

Rule#29

I undertake to receive alms-food in proportion (for example, one part of curry, three rice parts).
This rule reminds one of always receiving food in proportion and being humble.

Rule#30

I undertake to receive alms-food without exceeding the inner trim.
This rule reminds one of always being mindful of receiving food with appreciation and respect instead of greediness.

Rule#31

I undertake to be well restrained when eating.
This rule reminds one to always being mindful of eating food with appreciation and respect.

Rule#32

I undertake to keep attention on the bowl when eating.
This rule reminds one to always being mindful of eating food with appreciation and respect.

Rule#33

I undertake to eat the food in order, not picky.
This rule reminds one to always being mindful of eating food properly.

Rule#34

I undertake to eat food in proportion (for example, one spoon of curry, three rice spoons).
This rule reminds one of always eating in proportion and being humble.

Rule#35

I undertake to abstain from eating from the top of a heap of food. I take food from a site.
This rule reminds one to be well-restrained in eating.

Rule#36

I undertake to abstain from hiding tasty food in order the get more.
This rule reminds one of always being mindful of eating food with appreciation and respect instead of greediness.

Rule#37

I undertake to abstain from asking for food if not sick.
This rule reminds one to abstain from being too lazy to go out for alms-food.

Rule#38

I undertake to abstain from looking at the fellow bowl with jealousy.
This rule reminds one to appreciate the food he has and refrain from falling into the trap of greed and desire.

<h1 style="text-align:center">Rule#39</h1>

I undertake to abstain from making a large lump of food.

This rule reminds one to be well-restrained in eating.

<h1 style="text-align:center">Rule#40</h1>

I undertake to make a lump of food suitable for a mouthful.

This rule reminds one to be well-restrained in eating.

<h1 style="text-align:center">Rule#41</h1>

I undertake to abstain from opening the mouth before the food arrives at the mouth.

This rule reminds one to be well-restrained in eating.

<h1 style="text-align:center">Rule#42</h1>

I undertake to abstain from putting the finger into the mouth.

This rule helps one maintain her composure with proper behavior.

<h1 style="text-align:center">Rule#43</h1>

I undertake to abstain from speaking while eating food.

This rule promotes respect and self-restraint through proper behavior.

Rule#44

I undertake to abstain from throwing the food into the mouth.

This rule promotes respect and self-restraint through proper behavior.

Rule#45

I undertake to abstain from biting off the food.

This rule promotes respect and self-restraint through proper behavior.

Rule#46

I undertake to abstain from stuffing out the cheeks with food.

This rule promotes respect and self-restraint through proper behavior.

Rule#47

I undertake to abstain from shaking off the food.

This rule promotes respect and self-restraint through proper behavior.

Rule#48

I undertake to abstain from scattering the food.

This rule promotes respect and self-restraint through proper behavior.

Rule#49

I undertake to abstain from letting the tongue out.
This rule promotes respect and self-restraint through proper behavior.

Rule#50

I undertake to abstain from making champing noise when eating.
This rule promotes respect and self-restraint through proper behavior.

Rule#51

I undertake to abstain from making a sucking noise when dinking.
This rule promotes respect and self-restraint through proper behavior.

Rule#52

I undertake to abstain from licking the hand.
This rule promotes respect and self-restraint through proper behavior.

Rule#53

I undertake to abstain from scraping the bowl.
This rule promotes respect and self-restraint through proper behavior.

Rule#54

I undertake to abstain from licking the lips.
This rule promotes respect and self-restraint through proper behavior.

Rule#55

I undertake to abstain from washing hands, which still had the food.
This rule helps one to be well-restrained after eating and to avoid wasting food.

Rule#56

I undertake to abstain from throw out bowl-washing water, which still had the food.
This rule helps one to be well-restrained after eating and to avoid wasting food.

Rule#57

I undertake to abstain from teaching the person holding the umbrella.
This rule maintains personal safety from a stranger.

Rule#58

I undertake to abstain from teaching the person holding the walking stick.
This rule maintains personal safety from a stranger.

Rule#59

I undertake to abstain from teaching the person holding the sharp tool.

This rule maintains personal safety from a stranger.

Rule#60

I undertake to abstain from teaching the person holding the weapon.

This rule maintains personal safety from a stranger.

Rule#61

I undertake to abstain from teaching the person wearing shoes.

This rule maintains the value of teaching. The instructor requires attention and respect from the listener.

Rule#62

I undertake to abstain from teaching the person wearing sandals.

This rule maintains the value of teaching. The instructor requires attention and respect from the listener.

Rule#63

I undertake to abstain from teaching the person in the vehicle.

This rule maintains the value of teaching. The instructor requires attention and respect from the listener.

Rule#64

I undertake to abstain from teaching the person who is lying down.

This rule maintains the value of teaching. The instructor requires attention and respect from the listener.

Rule#65

I undertake to abstain from teaching the person sitting with the knees raised and the arms wrapped around the legs.

This rule maintains the value of teaching. The instructor requires attention and respect from the listener.

Rule#66

I undertake to abstain from teaching the person wearing a hat.

This rule maintains the value of teaching. The instructor requires attention and respect from the listener.

Rule#67

I undertake to abstain from teaching the person wearing the scarf to cover the head.

This rule maintains the value of teaching. The instructor requires attention and respect from the listener.

Rule#68

I undertake to abstain from teaching the person sitting on the seat while I'm sitting on the ground.
This rule maintains the value of teaching. The instructor requires attention and respect from the listener.

Rule#69

I undertake to abstain from teaching the person sitting on the high chair while I'm sitting on a lower chair.
This rule maintains the value of teaching. The instructor requires attention and respect from the listener.

Rule#70

I undertake to abstain from teaching the person who is sitting while I'm standing.
This rule maintains the value of teaching. The instructor requires attention and respect from the listener.

Rule#71

I undertake to abstain from teaching the person who is walking ahead.
This rule maintains the value of teaching. The instructor requires attention and respect from the listener.

Rule#72

I undertake to abstain from teaching the person walking on the pathway while I walk on the sideway.
This rule maintains the value of teaching. The instructor requires attention and respect from the listener.

Rule#73

I undertake to abstain from defecating or urinating while standing.
This rule preserves modesty.

Rule#74

I undertake to abstain from defecating or urinating, or spitting on the living plants.
All life is sacred, including plants. They, therefore, deserve to be respected.

Rule#75

I undertake to abstain from defecating or urinating, or spitting into the water.
This rule prevents one from contaminating water fit for drinking or bathing. Not only does it promote good hygiene and healthy living, but it is also a matter of respect.

The verdict

1. The administrator should give the verdict face to face.

This rule promotes honest verdicts and makes the nun accountable for her actions.

2. If the nun is innocent, the verdict should be "mindfulness."

Mindfulness is a way of life for those in the monastic community and should always be adopted.

3. If the nun was out of mind when she committed the offense, the verdict should be "past insanity."

This rule protects nuns who are temporarily insane.

4. If the nun confesses to the offense, the verdict should be "following what was admitted."

Confessing to a crime is a form of honesty, which is promoted in monastic life.

5. In some cases, the majority vote of administrators can decide on the case.

Using a majority vote of administrators to poll all those involved is a valuable tool, especially in cases that influence everyone.

6. **If the nun confesses after interrogation, the verdict should go further.**

Despite the honesty of a confession, interrogations should be pursued to determine an account of what happened and how it should be dealt with.

7. **If both nuns settled the dispute and admitted the mistakes. The administrator should give the verdict, "covering over as with grass."**

At this point, the dispute has been handled, and the decision should be met with respect.

110 additional rules for the nun

Rule#1

I undertake to abstain from associating with the monk who was guilty of severe misconduct.
This rule protects nuns from assumptions of misconduct.

Rule#2

I undertake to abstain from verbally or physically contacting or exposing my body to a man with lust.
This rule helps maintain chastity and prevents sexual misconduct with those of the opposite sex.

Rule#3

I undertake to abstain from arguing with laypeople.
This rule promotes peace and understanding with laypeople.

Rule#4

I undertake to abstain from accepting the female criminal as a novice.
This rule protects nuns from assumptions of misconduct.

Rule#5

I undertake to abstain from walking alone.
This rule promotes personal safety for the nun.

Rule#6

I undertake to abstain from forgiving the fellow who violates the code of conduct without administrator approval.

This rule maintains the importance of the proper functioning of the monastery and makes the monk accountable for his actions.

Rule#7

I undertake to abstain from receiving food from a man and eat with lust.

This rule helps maintain chastity and prevents sexual misconduct with those of the opposite sex.

Rule#8

I undertake to abstain from saying to the fellow," what does it matter to you whether the man is lustful or not? take the food and feed," as long as you are not lustful.

It is important to remain above suspicion by keeping oneself separate from any interactions with those of the opposite sex that could cause sexual misconduct or its assumption.

Rule#9

I undertake to abstain from defying the code of conduct training.

This rule maintains the importance of the proper functioning of the monastery and should be observed.

Rule#10

The nun who was angry over a minor offense should be warned three times before the administrator takes action.

This rule maintains the importance of the proper functioning of the monastery and should be observed.

Rule#11

The nun who lived in a group and committed a minor offense should be isolated. Later, if the nun still repeats it, she should be warned three times before the administrator takes action.

This rule maintains the importance of the proper functioning of the monastery and should be observed.

Rule#12

The nun who ignored the code of conduct and encouraged the others to do so as well should be warned three times before the administrator takes action.

This rule maintains the importance of the proper functioning of the monastery and should be observed.

Rule#13

I undertake to abstain from improperly using the robe.

This rule keeps one looking proper and humble.

Rule#14

I undertake to abstain from requesting the item, then returning it, and later requesting it again.
This rule supports the importance of honesty and proper behavior in monastic life.

Rule#15

I undertake to abstain from buying the item, then returning it, and later repurchasing it.
This rule supports the importance of honesty and proper behavior in monastic life.

Rule#16

I undertake to abstain from diverting the fund for the monastery to buy something else.
This rule supports the importance of honesty and proper behavior in monastic life.

Rule#17

I undertake to abstain from asking the fund for the monastery to buy something else.
This rule supports the importance of honesty and proper behavior in monastic life.

Rule#18

I undertake to abstain from diverting the fund for the group to buy something else.
This rule supports the importance of honesty and proper behavior in monastic life.

Rule#19

I undertake to abstain from asking the fund for the group to buy something else.
This rule supports the importance of honesty and proper behavior in monastic life.

Rule#20

I undertake to abstain from asking the fund for my fellow to buy something else.
This rule supports the importance of honesty and proper behavior in monastic life.

Rule#21

I undertake to abstain from asking for expensive thick cloth.
This rule prevents attachment to materials.

Rule#22

I undertake to abstain from asking for expensive thin cloth.
This rule prevents attachment to materials.

Rule#23

I undertake to abstain from eating garlic.
This rule prevents bad breath. Since nuns live in such close contact with each other and the community, it is thoughtful for them to refrain from eating strong foods that create a powerful odor.

Rule#24

I undertake to abstain from shaving the armpit and genital area.
This maintains a natural appearance and prevents attachment to the physical self or impure sexual thoughts.

Rule#25

I undertake to abstain from bringing water or fan to the monk who is eating.
This rule helps maintain chastity and prevents sexual misconduct or the possible assumption of it with those of the opposite sex.

Rule#26

I undertake to abstain from cooking the raw grain, nor ask someone.
This rule applies to all living beings, not just humans. All life is sacred, including raw grain, which will grow like plants. They, therefore, deserve to be respected.

Rule#27

I undertake to abstain from throwing the trash over the wall or fence, nor ask someone.

This rule protects modesty.

Rule#28

I undertake to abstain from throwing the trash over the living plants, nor ask someone.

All life is sacred, including plants. They, therefore, deserve to be respected.

Rule#29

I undertake to abstain from attending the entertainment show.

This rule instructs one to refrain from frivolous activities and aids in staying humble, mindful.

Rule#30

I undertake to abstain from talking to a man one on one in the dark.

This rule helps maintain chastity and prevents sexual misconduct or the possible assumption of it with those of the opposite sex.

Rule#31

I undertake to abstain from talking to a man one on one in the private room.

This rule helps maintain chastity and prevents sexual misconduct or the possible assumption of it with those of the opposite sex.

Rule#32

I undertake to abstain from talking to a man one on one in public.

This rule helps maintain chastity and prevents sexual misconduct or the possible assumption of it with those of the opposite sex.

Rule#33

I undertake to abstain from whispering to a man one on one in public.

This rule helps maintain chastity and prevents sexual misconduct or the possible assumption of it with those of the opposite sex.

Rule#34

I undertake to abstain from visiting the laypeople's residence before their mealtime.

This rule prevents the exploitation of laypeople.

Rule#35

I undertake to abstain from visiting the laypeople's residence in the afternoon or sunset without their permission.

This rule prevents the exploitation of laypeople.

Rule#36

I undertake to abstain from sleeping at the laypeople's residence without their permission.

This rule prevents the exploitation of laypeople.

Rule#37

I undertake to abstain from slandering the fellow.

This rule helps maintain peace and harmony in the monastery.

Rule#38

I undertake to abstain from cursing oneself or the fellow.

This rule helps maintain peace and harmony in the monastery.

Rule#39

I undertake to abstain from physically and emotionally abusing myself.

All life is sacred; this includes their own lives as well. This rule reminds us that everyone, including the self, should be cared for and respected.

Rule#40

I undertake to abstain from taking a bath naked.

This rule protects modesty.

Rule#41

I undertake to abstain from keeping the fellow's un-sewed cloth intended for a robe for more than 5 days.

This rule prevents procrastination.

Rule#42

I undertake to abstain from keeping the unsewed cloth intended for a robe for more than 5 days.

This rule prevents procrastination.

Rule#43

I undertake to abstain from using the fellow robe without her permission.

This rule promotes respect for others.

Rule#44

I undertake to abstain from interfering with the fellow receiving the robe cloth.

This rule helps maintain peace and harmony in the monastery.

Rule#45

I undertake to abstain from blocking the robe cloth distribution.

This rule maintains the importance of the proper functioning of the monastery and should be respected.

Rule#46

I undertake to abstain from giving the marked robe to laypeople.

This rule preserves the sanctity of what the robe represents, which is the dedication to monastic life.

Rule#47

I undertake to abstain from skipping the robe season.

This rule maintains the importance of the proper functioning of the monastery and should be respected.

Rule#48

I undertake to abstain from dismantling the robe season.

This rule maintains the importance of the proper functioning of the monastery and should be respected.

Rule#49

I undertake to abstain from sleeping with the fellow in a single bed.

This rule prevents sexual misconduct among fellows.

Rule#50

I undertake to abstain from sleeping with the fellow in a single blanket.

This rule prevents sexual misconduct among fellows.

Rule#51

I undertake to abstain from annoying the fellow.

This rule promotes peace and harmony among fellows.

Rule#52

I undertake to abstain from not visiting the sick student.

This rule promotes compassion for those living in the monastery.

Rule#53

I undertake to abstain from expelling the roommate.

This rule promotes peace and harmony among fellows.

Rule#54

I undertake to abstain from living with laypeople.

This rule prevents the exploitation of laypeople.

Rule#55

I undertake to abstain from walking alone in an unsafe local area.

This rule protects the safety of nuns.

Rule#56

I undertake to abstain from walking alone in an unsafe distant area.

This rule protects the safety of nuns.

Rule#57

I undertake to abstain from missing the rains retreat during the rainy season.

This rule maintains the importance of the proper functioning of the monastery and should be respected.

Rule#58

I undertake to abstain from going farther than 125km after completing the rains retreat.

This rule protects the safety of nuns.

Rule#59

I undertake to abstain from visiting the amusement center.

This rule instructs one to refrain from frivolous activities and aids in staying humble, mindful.

Rule#60

I undertake to abstain from using the high platform.

This rule maintains humility.

Rule#61

I undertake to abstain from doing textile work.

Those in the monastic community have their basic needs met. Therefore, they no need to earn money to purchase food and other needed items; they pursue the spiritual path. In fact, textile work would only be a distraction that would detract from their focused lives of mindfulness.

Rule#62

I undertake to abstain from doing the daily work for laypeople.

Those in the monastic community have their basic needs met. Therefore, they no need to earn money to purchase food and other needed items; they pursue the spiritual path. In fact, daily work would only be a distraction that would detract from their focused mindfulness lives.

Rule#63

I undertake to abstain from involving myself in the disputes as a referee.

This rule maintains the importance of the proper functioning of the monastery and maintains peace and harmony.

Rule#64

I undertake to abstain from leaving menstrual cloths behind after using.

This rule protects modesty.

Rule#65

I undertake to abstain from learning the art.
Those in the monastic community have their basic needs met. They pursue the spiritual path. In fact, learning the art would only be a distraction that would detract from their focused mindfulness lives.

Rule#66

I undertake to abstain from teaching art.
Those in the monastic community have their basic needs met. Therefore, they no need to earn money to purchase food and other needed items; they pursue the spiritual path. In fact, teaching art would only be a distraction that would detract from their focused mindfulness lives.

Rule#67

I undertake to abstain from insulting the monk.
This rule promotes peace and harmony among fellows.

Rule#68

I undertake to abstain from insulting the community of nuns.
This rule promotes peace and harmony among fellows.

Rule#69

I undertake to abstain from being stingy to my family (supporter).
This rule promotes compassion and appreciation.

Rule#70

I undertake to abstain from staying in the monastery without a monk during the rains retreat.
This rule promotes personal safety for nuns.

Rule#71

I undertake to abstain from criticizing the monks or nuns without clear evidence of misconduct during the rains retreat.
This rule helps maintain peace and harmony in the monastery.

Rule#72

I undertake to attend the observance day for counseling.
This rule maintains the importance of the proper functioning of the monastery and should be respected.

Rule#73

Every two weeks, I undertake to ask the monk community two things: the date of observance day and the counseling.
This rule maintains the importance of the proper functioning of the monastery and should be respected.

Rule#74

I undertake to abstain from taking care of the man with a genital area injury alone without the administrator's permission.

This rule avoids any potential for or suspicions of misconduct with those of the opposite sex.

Rule#75

I undertake to abstain from accepting the pregnant woman(as a novice).

One who is pregnant does not have the focus required to dedicate herself to monastic life.

Rule#76

I undertake to abstain from accepting (as a novice) the woman who is still nursing the baby.

One with a young nursling does not have the focus required to dedicate herself to monastic life.

Rule#77

I undertake to abstain from accepting the woman who never observed the six precepts (the first six of eight precepts) for two years.

The six precepts layout an important foundation for morality and good living. One who has not followed this path is not prepared for monastic life.

Rule#78

I undertake to abstain from accepting the woman who never observed the six precepts (the first six of eight precepts) for two years nor approved by the administrator.

The six precepts layout an important foundation for morality and good living. One who has not followed this path or has not been approved by the administrator is not prepared for monastic life.

Rule#79

I undertake to abstain from accepting the (under 12 years old) married woman who never observed the six precepts (the first six of eight precepts) for two years.

The six precepts layout an important foundation for morality and good living. One who has not followed this path is not prepared for monastic life.

Rule#80

I undertake to abstain from accepting the (12 years old) married woman who never observed the six precepts (the first six of eight precepts) for two years nor approved by the administrator.

The six precepts layout an important foundation for morality and good living. One who has not followed this path or has not been approved by the administrator is not prepared for monastic life.

Rule#81

I undertake to abstain from accepting the student whom I will not train for the next two years.
Taking a student under one's training is a huge responsibility and should not be taken lightly. This rule helps students receive adequate training.

Rule#82

I undertake to abstain from ignoring the preceptor for two years.
This rule promotes respect, gratitude, and compassion to the preceptor.

Rule#83

I undertake to abstain from accepting the student who never goes 125km or more away.
This rule prevents the acceptance of trainees without qualification.

Rule#84

I undertake to abstain from accepting the (20 years old and single) trainee who never observed the six precepts (the first six of eight precepts) for two years.
The six precepts layout an important foundation for morality and good living. One who has not followed this path is not prepared for monastic life.

Rule#85

I undertake to abstain from accepting the (20 years old and single) trainee who never observed the six precepts (the first six of eight precepts) for two years nor approved by the administrator.

The six precepts layout an important foundation for morality and good living. One who has not followed this path or has not been approved by the administrator is not prepared for monastic life.

Rule#86

I undertake to abstain from accepting a trainee who is under 12 years of age.

Monastic life requires dedication, focus, and hard work that is beyond the capabilities of a child. It also prevents the acceptance of trainees who are not prepared for monastic life.

Rule#87

I undertake to abstain from accepting a trainee under the age of 12 and not approved by the administrator.

Monastic life requires dedication, focus, and hard work that is beyond the capabilities of a child or has not been approved by the administrator is not prepared for monastic life.

Rule#88

I undertake to abstain from flip-flopping the acceptance.

This rule upholds the honesty of the acceptance of trainees.

Rule#89

I undertake to abstain from accepting the trainee by bribery.

This rule upholds honesty and prevents the acceptance of trainees without qualification.

Rule#90

I undertake to abstain from lying about the acceptance to the trainee.

This rule upholds the honesty of the acceptance of trainees.

Rule#91

I undertake to abstain from accepting the trainee who has a relationship with a boy or group of youth.

This rule prevents the acceptance of trainees who are not prepared for monastic life.

Rule#92

I undertake to abstain from accepting a trainee without permission from their parent or husband.
This rule prevents the acceptance of trainees without approval from their families.

Rule#93

I undertake to abstain from accepting a trainee without the state approval.
This rule prevents the acceptance of trainees without qualification.

Rule#94

I undertake to abstain from acting as a preceptor and accepting the trainee in consecutive years.
This rule prevents the acceptance of trainees for personal satisfaction.

Rule#95

I undertake to abstain from acting as a preceptor and accepting two trainees in one year.
This rule prevents the acceptance of trainees for personal satisfaction.

Rule#96

I undertake to abstain from using shoe or leather footwear, if not ill.

This rule promotes humility and prevents attachment to materials.

Rule#97

I undertake to abstain from riding in a vehicle for a close distance, if not ill.

This rule promotes humility and prevents attachment to personal comfort.

Rule#98

I undertake to abstain from wearing hip ornament.

This rule promotes humility and prevents attachment to materials.

Rule#99

I undertake to abstain from wearing a woman's ornament.

This rule promotes humility and prevents attachment to materials.

Rule#100

I undertake to abstain from taking a bath with herb or scents, if not ill.

This rule promotes humility and prevents attachment to personal comfort.

Rule#101

I undertake to abstain from taking a bath with scented sesame powder, if not ill.
This rule promotes humility and prevents attachment to personal comfort.

Rule#102

I undertake to abstain from receiving a massage by the fellow.
This rule prevents sexual misconduct among fellows.

Rule#103

I undertake to abstain from receiving a massage from the trainee.
This rule prevents sexual misconduct among instructors and trainees.

Rule#104

I undertake to abstain from massaging by the female novice.
This rule prevents sexual misconduct.

Rule#105

I undertake to abstain from massaging by the lay-woman.
This rule prevents sexual misconduct.

Rule#106

I undertake to abstain from sitting down in front of a monk without asking for his permission.

This rule promotes respect through proper action.

Rule#107

I undertake to abstain from counseling the monk.

This rule avoids any potential for or suspicions of misconduct with those of the opposite sex.

Rule#108

I undertake to abstain from entering the village without a vest.

This rule preserves modesty.

Rule#109

I undertake to abstain from standing on tiptoes or the heels in public.

This rule helps one maintain her composure with proper behavior.

Rule#110

I undertake to abstain from sitting without clasping the knees in public.

This rule preserves modesty